RECOVERY & LIFE COACHING
THE OFFICIAL WORKBOOK
FOR COACHES AND THEIR CLIENTS

Written by Rev. Dr. Kevin T. Coughlin Ph.D. & Dr. Cali Estes Ph.D.

RECOVERY & LIFE COACHING THE OFFICIAL WORKBOOK
FOR COACHES AND THEIR CLIENTS

Written by Rev. Dr. Kevin T. Coughlin PhD. & Dr. Cali Estes Ph.D.

KTC Publishing Phase IIC Coaching, LLC

This book is a work of nonfiction.

First Printing

Copyright © 2016 Rev. Dr. Kevin T. Coughlin Ph.D. & Dr. Cali Estes Ph.D.

KTC Publishing Phase IIC Coaching, LLC

All Rights Reserved.

As permitted under the US Copyright Act of 1976, no part of this publication may be reproduced, distributed, or transmitted in any form or by any means (electronic, mechanical, photocopying, recording, or otherwise, stored in a database or retrieval system, without prior written permission of the copyright holder of this book, except by a reviewer, who may quote brief passages in a review.

The scanning, uploading, and distribution of this book via the Internet or other means without the written permission of the copyright holder and publisher is illegal and punishable by law. Please purchase only authorized electronic editions, and do not participate in or encourage electronic piracy of copyrighted materials. Your support of the author is appreciated.

Printed in the United States of America

ISBN 978-0-9977006-6-4 (paperback)

Recovery Coaching, The Official Workbook has been used successfully by numerous individuals, residential recovery programs, out-patient programs, professional recovery coaches, aftercare professionals, counselors, therapists, probation officers, ministries, recovery retreats, sponsors, sober companions, and family members to help them to get a deeper understanding of the disease of addiction, the solution to the problem, and the program of action that promotes change in the substance abuser. A Support system for family and friends of substance abusers that help to provide clarity, understanding, education, prevention, and awareness.

Please, visit www.theaddiction.expert & www.theaddictionscoach.com for other books written and published by Rev. Dr. Kevin T. Coughlin Ph.D. and Dr. Cali Estes Ph.D., there you can join their mailing lists for advanced notice on their next books, training, and live events.

Disclaimer: In this book, the author shares his experience, strength, and hope with readers, this should not be considered advice. All information in this book is for informational and educational purposes, not medical or psychiatric advice or to prescribe the use of any technique as a form of treatment for medical or psychiatric problems without the advice of a physician, psychiatrist or appropriate licensed professional either directly or indirectly. In the event, you use any of the information in this book for yourself, neither the authors nor the publisher accepts responsibility for your actions.

Introduction

Rev. Dr. Kevin T. Coughlin Ph.D. was a Founder and Board Member of a Residential Recovery Facility New Beginning Ministry, Inc. a program for men and women struggling with life and addiction problems, and the Founder and CEO of Phase IIC Coaching, LLC, a recovery coaching, life coaching, intervention, and addiction education, awareness, and prevention company. Rev. Dr. Coughlin has been helping to change and save thousands of lives for over two decades. He is a prolific writer, author, poet, speaker, consultant, Master coach, interventionist, Christian therapist, Pastoral Counselor and expert on addiction.

Dr. Cali Estes Ph.D. is the Founder and CEO of The Addictions Academy and The Addictions Coach of Miami, Florida. At The Addictions Coach, Dr. Estes works with clients to help them overcome life and addiction problems. Cali Estes is an interactive, solution-focused Master Addictions Counselor (MAC) and Master Certified Addiction Professional (MCAP), coach and mentor. Her therapeutic approach is to provide support and practical feedback to help clients effectively address personal life challenges. The Addictions Academy offers International Certifications and Courses in Recovery Coaching, Intervention, Anger Management, Food Addictions, Family Recovery Coaching and other Certifications to Professionals. She is a sought after Counselor, Addictions Coach, and Life Coach to Actors, Musicians, CEO's, Doctors, Sports Figures and Attorneys that need 100% Confidentiality.

Rev. Dr. Coughlin joined Dr. Estes at The Addictions Academy as the program Director in 2014. The two noticed that there was a great need for a workbook for coaches and their clients that were both practical and fun to utilize. The rest is history! The workbook was outlined and written over an eighteen-month period. The workbook proof was evaluated by some of the Addictions Academy's students and their clients; the results were amazing! Everyone wanted a copy; however, the official workbook was still in production. The version of the workbook that you have purchased is tried, tested, and proven as a winner!

This workbook for coaches and their clients should be a tool in every coach's office and briefcase. If you're a coach, and you don't have this workbook, you are missing out! If you're a client, and your coach doesn't use this workbook, you're missing out! We know that coaches and their clients everywhere will benefit from this tremendous workbook.

We would like to thank all of the Addictions Academy Alumni who were involved in testing this workbook with their clients in the field, and giving us honest feedback. Without our alumni's help, we may not have seen the potential and need for this wonderful workbook for coaches and their clients. Coaching should be life changing, results and client driven, and solution focused. This workbook will aid coaches everywhere to help their clients to change their perceptions and perspectives and take the action necessary to get results.

Thank you for purchasing our workbook! Don't forget to celebrate all of the victories along your journey; this is one of them!

Professional Recovery Coaching and Sober Companions have dedicated their lives to helping those still sick and suffering from the insidious, cunning, baffling, and powerful disease of addiction find solutions. Recovery coaching is client and goal driven, where coaches utilize specialized tools, skill sets, and core competencies to help the client to change perspectives and perceptions and find solutions that were unobtainable to them in the past. Professional Coaches do not conduct process work, they leave that for counselors and therapists. Coaches stay focused on today and moving forward. Coaches set a solid foundation with clients through professional standards and ethical guidelines, establishing an agreement with their clients and establishing a presence and relationship based on trust and intimacy. Professional recovery coaches are expert communicators utilizing active listening, powerful questioning, and direct communication to assist in creating client awareness, goal setting, and designing action plans, and then managing the client's progress while holding them accountable. Coaches demonstrate flexibility, creativity, understanding, and compassion, and celebrate all the victories along the road to success with their clients. Professional recovery coaches partner with clients in a thought-provoking process that is designed to be creative and inspirational so that clients maximize their lives potential and promise. Ultimately coaches set clients up for success!

Table of Contents

Table of Contents

Introduction	5
Table of Contents	7
The Professional Recovery Coach's Questionnaire and Forms	8
Drug and Alcohol Questionnaire	17
Report Writing:	23
ACTION PLAN	24
The Disease of Addiction and Diagrams on Addiction and Recovery:	26
Personal Stress Scale	34
Goal Setting	38
Random Acts of Kindness	40
NOTES:	43
Life Impact:	44
Treat Yourself Better Exercise	45
Insomnia Due to Anxiety Exercise	46
Self-esteem Collage Board	47
My Self-esteem Calendar	48
Confidence Building Exercise	49
Resources	1
Rev. Dr. Kevin T. Coughlin Ph.D. Publication Credits	3
About The Authors	6

The Professional Recovery Coach's Questionnaire and Forms

Coach introduction: good morning, afternoon, or evening, my name is _____
thank you for calling/ coming in today. I appreciate your time.
Do you have any questions before we get started? If yes, answer briefly. If no, move on.

(Questions)

Last name: _____, Middle: _____, First: _____
What is your date of birth? ___/___/____   Age: _____
Address: _____
Phone Number: (___)-____-_____ Cell Number: (___)-_____-_____
Emergency Contact: name: _____ Phone Number: (___)-_____-_____   Relationship: _____ 2nd Number: (___)-_____-_____
How did you hear about my company? __Friend, __Website, __Ad, __Article, __Referral   Referred by: _____.
What is your main goal in coming to see me today? _____   What have you specifically done about the problem yourself?   _____

Referral Resources (Circle all that apply)

Self-referral	Court	Therapist
Church/clergy	Corrections	Family Friend
Treatment Provider	Family	Recovery Support Services
School	Child Welfare	Employer
Physician	Counselor	Other

How do you feel about being here today? (Circle all that apply)

Angry	Uncertain	Hopeful
Resentful	Reserved	Happy
Anxious	Resigned	Excited
Fearful	Afraid	Determined
Scared	Confused	Ready

What would you like to accomplish through coaching? (Circle all that apply)

Maintain Sobriety	Get Employment	Obtain Housing
Recovery Support	Child Custody	Food/Clothing
Meet Legal Requirements	Improve Relationships	Avoid Jail/Prison
Anger Management	Get Partner/Spouse Back	Recovery Network
Become More Spiritual	Improve Life	Become Better Person
Understand Addiction	Understand Recovery	Change Thinking
More Service Work	Get Sponsor	Change How I Live
Go to AA/NA meetings	Pray/Meditate More	Other

Please list you most important goals in order of importance to you.

1.	2.	3.	4.
5.	6.	7.	8.

On a scale of 1-5 with (5) being very confident and (1) being not confident, how confident are you that you will be able to achieve each one of your listed goals?

Please place the corresponding number in each box.

1.	2.	3.	4.
5.	6.	7.	8.

On the same scale, how ready are you to start working on your goals today?

Please place the corresponding number in each box.

1.	2.	3.	4.
5.	6.	7.	8.

Please circle all that apply to you.

If you have an emergency situation and need help, call 911.

1. Not Safe At Home	2. Suicidal	3. Abused	4. Risk of Relapse
5. Homeless	6. No Food	7. Mental Health	8. No Medication
9. Sexual Abuse	10. Special Needs	11. Not Safe In Neighborhood	12. Need Medical Attention

EMERGENCIES CALL 911
National Suicide Prevention Lifeline
1-800-273-8255

Please check the boxes that apply to you for transportation.

	Valid License to Drive		License Suspended		Need Help to Get License to Drive		Need Funds to Get License
	Own a Car		Don't Have a Car		Family Has Car		Want to Buy a Used Car
	Public Transportation		Don't Have a Bus Pass		Have a Bus Pass		Need Help With Funds
	Ride a Bike		Need a Bike		Bike Needs Repair		Need Funds to Repair Bike
	Walk to Where I Need to Go		Disabled Can't Walk		Need Comfortable Walking Shoes		No Funds for Shoes

Please circle any special transportation needs you may have.

Special Needs Hearing Impairment	Special Needs Visual Impairment	Need Wheelchair/Handicap Access
Special Needs Due to Physical Mobility Restrictions	Walk With Assistance Cane/ Walker	Other (specify) _____

Please circle anything that relates to your current employment status.

Are you employed?	Full-time student	Work part-time irregular hours
Laid off	Someone supports me	In the military
Terminated	Retired	Volunteer work only
Quit job	Disabled	Like my job/ don't like job
Out of work over 90 days	Can't find wok/legal problems	Looking for a new job
Looking for work	Just got out of jail	I have more than 1 job
Want to work/can't find job	Work full-time 35+ hours	My job is good for recovery, my job is bad for my recovery
Choose not to work	Work part-time reg. hours	Job does not affect my recovery

Circle all job skills that apply to you.

1. Child Care	2. Trucking	3. Business	4. Professional
5. Customer Service	6. Health Care	7. Sales	8. Office
9. Trade	10. Landscaping	11. Supervision	12. Other

Think of the job skills that you have.

List them in order of what is your best skill from 1-12, 1 being your best, 12 being your worst.

1.	2.	3.	4.
5.	6.	7.	8.
9.	10.	11.	12.

List 8 skills that you would like to develop and get more experience in.

1.	2.	3.	4.
5.	6.	7.	8.

Please circle all the responsibilities that you have outside of work.

Child Care	Care for Disabled Family	Housework/ Chores	School and Homework
Care for Elderly Family	Mandatory Reporting Probation	Report to Case Manager	Take Care of Pets
Mandatory AA/NA Meetings	Report to Out Patient	Step Work with Sponsor	Parole Requirements

Do you think it would benefit you to get some help with employment/work related matters? y/n

Circle the type of help that you would like.

Bettor Job	Improve Interviewing Skills	Vocational Assessment
Developing Job Skills	Develop Resume	Help Finding Work
Disability Evaluation	Promotions	Maintain Job
Disability Work Rehabilitation	Interviewing Skills Arrange Interviews	Barriers Related to Felony Convictions

Please circle your education level.

High School Diploma	College No Diploma	Bachelor's BA, BUS
High School didn't finish	College 1 year, 3 years	Master's Degree MA, MS
High School/GED Voc/Tech Diploma after High School	College Associates Degree AA, AS	Doctorate multiple doctorates

Please list certifications and training.

Are you a student now or in any specialized training? y/n

Please circle any item that you're interested in getting help with.

Earn GED	Academic Counseling	Tutoring
Literacy Training	Aptitude/Achievement Tests	Grants/Loans for School
Returning to school additional training	Technical/Vocational Training	Applying to schools other: _____

Please circle who you live with.

With Spouse/Domestic Partner and Children	With Spouse/Domestic Partner	With Child/Children	With Parent/Parents
With Other Family	With Friends	Alone	Controlled
Homeless	Temporary	Group Home	Other: _____

Please circle all that apply to your living situation.

If any question makes you uncomfortable, leave it out.

People Support Recovery	Threatening	My neighborhood is safe
People are in Recovery	Intimidating	Neighborhood not safe
People do not Support	Verbally Abusive	Neighborhood is dangerous
People keep drugs in house	Physically Abusive	Not dangerous
People keep alcohol in house	Sexually Abusive	Good for recovery
People use drugs and alcohol	I am safe in house	Bad for recovery
People sell drugs	I am not safe in house	Would like to move
People discourage my recovery	Family safe, family not safe	Would like to stay

Circle any of these you may be interested in.

Emergency Housing	Temp Housing	Recovery Home	Stable Housing
Supported independent living	Help finding Subsidized Housing	Oxford House, other clean and Sober Housing	Housing barriers related to felons

Have you experienced any legal trouble?

If yes, circle all that apply to you.

Ever been arrested	DUI arrest	PTA	Parole
Convicted felony	DUI conviction	AR program/ fines	Probation
Misdemeanor	Jail time/ prison time	Child Support	Active Warrants
Charges dropped	Community Service hours due	Public Defender/ paid attorney	Awaiting trial

Please describe your mental health history below.

Mental Health diagnosis y/n?	What is your mh diagnosis? _____	Are you prescribed any medications for mh issues? y/n
Have you ever been hospitalized because of mh reason? y/n		II yes, what are they? _____
If yes, where and why?	Have you ever had detox complications? y/n	Have you ever had treatment for addiction? y/n?
Where:	If yes, what?	If yes, where?
Why:		

Circle the statement that best describes your current situation.

I don't have an addiction problem.	I'm in recovery and have been drug and alcohol-free for over 1 year.	I'm in early recovery and have been clean and sober for 90 days.
I haven't used in 1 week.	I have used in the last week.	I'm actively using.
I want to stop using but can't stop.	I don't want to stop.	I'm court ordered to stop.

Please answer the questions below as they relate to you.

Do you have a recovery plan? y/n	Do you want help to create a recovery action plan? y/n
Do you want help to update your recovery plan? y/n	Who if anyone is helping you meet current recovery goals? sponsor, case manager, recovery coach, recovery support services, or other: _____
What person do you look to when you need help? _____	Are you interested in working with a trained professional who can help you to reach your recovery goals and solutions? y/n

I have listed 8 sober activities that you could do; please list 8 of your own.

1. Writing/poetry	5. Lifting weights	9.	13.
2. Walking	6. Bowling	10.	14.
3. Music	7. Hiking	11.	15.
4. Art	8. Gardening	12.	16.

Please circle all items that apply to you that you may need assistance with.

Bankruptcy 7,13	Alimony	Debt	Discrimination
Criminal Record	Child Support	No Health Insurance	Disability
Immigration Status	No income	Paying for meds	Getting divorced
Child Custody	Child Custody Pay	Alimony Pay	Probation problems
Legal Defense	Need food stamps	Need clothing	Need personal items
Need detox	Need treatment	Need housing paid	Need heating paid
Need diapers	Need a phone	Need money	Need child care
Need help reading	Can't speak English	Need a mentor	Need help

Anger Log

Date	Angry at?	Why I am angry and what I did about it? (Positive or Negative behavior.)	P/N

Aftercare Needs Form

Client	Date	Time	Agency	Address	Trans
John Doe	1/1/14	1500	Parole	Main St. Allentown	Needs

Chairperson sign	Date	NA/AA	Signature	Date	Agency	Time
Signed by Chairperson	1/1/14	NA	Officer Blue Signs	1/1/14	State Parole	1600
"Ditto"	1/15/14	AA				
"Ditto"	1/16/14	AA				
"Ditto"	1/17/14	AA				
"Ditto"	1/18/14	NA				
"Ditto"	1/19/14	NA				

Check off areas that pertain to your client. Appointment dates and time are written on top.

Client	Agency	Date	Time	Agency	Date	Time	Agency	Date	Time
J. Doe	Parole	1/1/14	1500						

X	Parole		Probation		Detox		Volunteer		Minor
X	Fines due		Therapy		Res. Treat.		Counseling	X	Transport
	Dental		Social Ser.		I.O.P.		Financial		Sponsor
	Doctor		Work		Rec Coach		Special Needs		Religion
	Housing		Pscsy.		School		Citizenship		Church
X	AA/NA/Rec.		Drive License		Family		Anger Manage		Memberships
	Child Support		Drug Court		Children		Intervention		Insurance
	Food		Clothing		Custody		Drug Testing		Surgery
	Medications		Legal		Hygiene		Court Order		Mental Health

Life Coaching Chart:

- 1. There are 98 hours in a week at 7 days a week 14 hours per day.
- 2. How much time does the client spend on the following areas each week?
- 3. Health. How important is their health to them?
- 4. Wealth. What does wealthy mean to the client?
- 5. Family. How important is family to them?
- 6. Relationships. How important are relationships and who are the important people?
- 7. Job/Career. What's important in client's work?
- 8. Spiritual. How important is spiritual growth?
- 9. Playtime. What does client do for fun?
- 10. Contribution. World contribution. How important?
- 11. What areas do you lack in? How important?

In each category what is client's current situation, how much time each week, and what is the client's future goals? You can make this into a chart if you choose.			
Health	1-2-3-4-5-6-7-8-9-10	Wky hrs:	
Wealth	1-2-3-4-5-6-7-8-9-10	Wky hrs:	
Relationships	1-2-3-4-5-6-7-8-9-10	Wky hrs:	
Family	1-2-3-4-5-6-7-8-9-10	Wky hrs:	
Career/Job	1-2-3-4-5-6-7-8-9-10	Wky hrs:	
Spiritual	1-2-3-4-5-6-7-8-9-10	Wky hrs:	
Playtime	1-2-3-4-5-6-7-8-9-10	Wky hrs:	
World	1-2-3-4-5-6-7-8-9-10	Wky hrs:	
Category	**importance 10 most**	**weekly hours**	**future goals**
Health	7	1	Want to improve
Wealth	10 being able	40	More wealth
Relationships	7	5 Out of	Improve
Family	8	7 Balance!	Improve
Career	10	45	Improve
Spiritual	10	0	Get more
Playtime	2	0	More
World	7	Overlaps	Improve

Drug and Alcohol Questionnaire

Client name: **Coach:**   **Date:**

Circle any drug that you have used, and explain first and last use, and if ever a problem:

Alcohol
Barbiturates
Sleeping pills
Benzodiazepines
Caffeine
Cocaine
Crack
Ecstasy (MDMA)
Ephedra
Gasoline
Glue
Heroin
Other Inhalants
LSD
Marijuana or Hashish
Methadone
Methamphetamine
Mescaline
Mushrooms
Nicotine
Nitrous Oxide
Opiates (pain pills)
Opium
PCP
Peyote
Poppers
Prescription Drugs
Psilocybin
Quaaludes
Seconaol (Reds)
Speedballs
Steroids
Tuinol (Yellows)

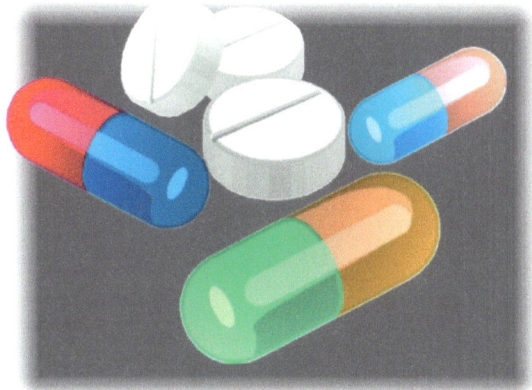

Please put a circle around any of the drugs above that you feel you are addicted to or dependent upon.

How did you get started using drugs/alcohol?

When you consume alcohol, what do you usually drink?

How many drinks do you usually have per day or per week?

How much (name of drug) do you usually have per day or per week?

How have you ingested (the drug)?

Swallow/Smoke/Sniff/Inject/Mix with other?

What is the best thing about getting high?

What is your favorite thing to do when drinking or using drugs?

Are there any times you tend to use these substances less?

Are there any times you have successfully stopped?

How much do you spend each week on your drugs/alcohol?

Do you usually drink/use drugs alone or with others?

At home or elsewhere?

What time of day do you usually start using drugs/drinking?

Is there a pattern to your use?

What effects does drinking/using drugs have on your feelings and emotions?

Do you or have you ever experienced any physical symptoms when you try to stop drinking or use drugs?

If so, which ones?   Shakes/tremors, sweating, seizures, continuous vomiting, sleeplessness, disorientation, hallucinations, depression, hypersomnia, increased appetite, other?

Do you gamble when you drink or use drugs?

Is your gambling out of control or excessive?

Have you ever had an eating disorder (bulimia, anorexia, obesity)?

Which family members have had a drug or alcohol problem (circle)?

How were you affected by your family member's drug abuse?

Does anyone in your household use drugs or drink?
If so, who?

Do most of your friends drink or use illicit drugs?

Please circle any problems that have persisted following your use of drugs or alcohol:

Hepatitis or liver problems, persistent cough, hallucinations, strange thoughts, congestion or wheezing, heart problems, depression, mania. Other:

Please circle any social or relationship problems that have resulted from your use of alcohol or drugs:

Arguments with spouse or partner, thrown out of house, social isolation, arguments with parents or siblings, loss of friends, spouse or partner left you, other:

Please circle any job or financial problems caused or worsened by your use of drugs or alcohol:

Lost a job, less productive at work, behind in paying bills, late to work, in debt, bankruptcy, foreclosure, repossession, missed days at work, missed opportunities for raise or promotion, other:

Please circle any problems caused or worsened by use of alcohol or drugs:

Arrest for possession, forging prescriptions, assault, embezzlement, forgery, selling drugs, driving under the influence, arson, sexual assault, hate crimes, homicide, theft or robbery.

Have you ever attended a twelve-step program?

Have you ever gone to an outpatient program for drugs or alcohol?

Have you ever been in an inpatient facility for drugs or alcohol?

Have you ever used a prescription medication to abstain from drinking or using drugs?

Have you ever had a drug overdose or alcohol poisoning?

Have you ever attempted suicide while intoxicated or using?

What is the longest period of not using you have had to date?

How have you stayed clean and sober so far?

What caused you to want to stop using?

What do you think the result will be if you keep using?

Please write a T if True and an F is False at the end of each question.

1. I drink/use drugs when I feel anxious.
2. I often try to hide or minimize my drinking/drug use.
3. Many of my friends drink or use Illicit drugs.
4. I have broken the law to support my habit.
5. I would never consider going to a 12-step program.
6. Drinking or using drugs has never really caused me any problems.
7. I have tried to stop using drugs/drinking in the past.
8. I drink/use drugs when I feel depressed.
9. When I drink, I usually get drunk.
10. I feel more confident when I drink or use drugs.
11. Sometimes I use drugs or drink in the morning.
12. Friends or family have told me I should stop drinking or using drugs.
13. I spend too much time thinking about drinking or using drugs.
14. I become very anxious if I am unable to have a drink or do drugs.
15. I have never stolen in order to buy drugs or alcohol.
16. I am an alcoholic.
17. I am a drug addict.
18. I have experienced the need to use more drugs to get the effect I had the first time I used them.
19. If I stopped using drugs or drinking, I would lose many of my friends.
20. I am not a religious person.
21. I think better when I have a few drinks or use drugs.
22. I think I have a problem with sexual or gambling addiction.
23. Drinking or using drugs helps me forget about my problems and relax.
24. I have never used drugs and alcohol at the same time.
25. I have sometimes alternated taking uppers and downers.

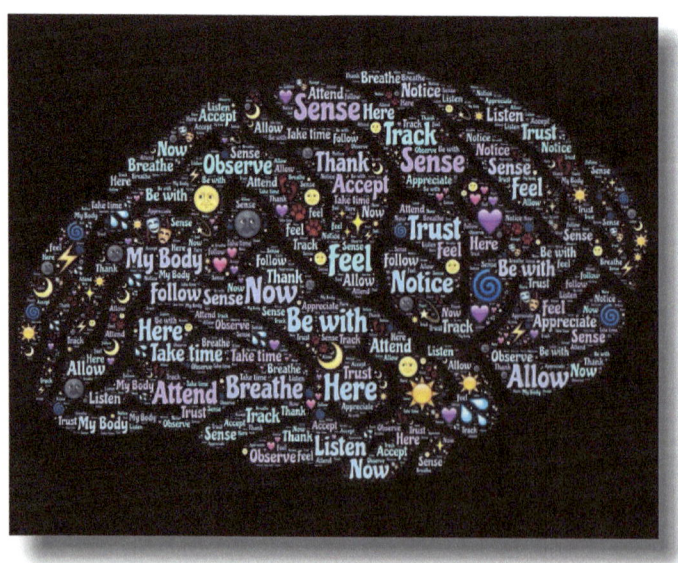

Have you ever experienced any of the following symptoms when you use drugs or alcohol? (circle)

Seizures
Blackouts
Hallucinations
Paranoia
Personality changes
Decreased need for sleep/ Increased aggression/Severe weight loss/ Ulcers/other stomach problems/Headaches/Excessive bleeding/ Sinus problems /Heart palpitations/Suicidal thoughts/Panic attacks/Memory problems/Depression/ Other:

This is the Life Pie Exercise
Divide your pie into eight even slices
at the crust label each of the eight slices
health, wealth, relationships, family, career/job, spiritual, playtime, world
then for each slice of pie divide it into 10ths from the center of the pie
the center would be one, then two, half way would be five, the crust would be ten.
Ask you client how important each area is in their life on a scale of 1 through ten
one being the least important and ten being the most important
have them shade the area around the pie that represents the important areas for center outward.

Report Writing:

The A, B, C s of Report Writing, be accurate, brief, and clear. Then the five Ws, Who, What, Why, When, Where, and How. When you write a report, an article, or an essay, don't try to sound important using big words. The best writers use words that an eighth grader can understand. Don't try to be someone that you're not, or sound like someone that you're not. Remember, as life coaches, we don't do process work. We go from today forward, never into the past. Let the therapists and Doctors do that! Never make a diagnosis! If you have to send a report to the court, probation, or parole, you can state, it is of my opinion that John needs long-term care. The key words are "it is of my opinion". You don't want to be in a situation where you get accused of diagnosing a client without the credentials or license to do so. Remember confidentiality! If you fall under HIPAA compliance guidelines, remember you have to know who a report is for and have a release to release any information that is protected by law.

Action Planning:

- ❖ Action plans need to be specific.
- ❖ Identify Goals and Objectives.
- ❖ How do you get from point A. to point B.?
- ❖ Who is going to assist you?
- ❖ Why do you need to do this action?
- ❖ Where are you going to do this action?
- ❖ What is the plan?
- ❖ Who will follow up?
- ❖ On what timetable, be specific?

Example:	
Goals and Objectives:	To Improve Communication with coworkers
How:	Clarify Expectations, Meetings
Why:	To Improve Teamwork and Consistency
Who:	John Clarify Expectations, Everyone at Meetings
Where:	XYZ Corp. Meeting Room
When:	Friday, August 22, 2014, 4PM.
Follow-up:	John and Coach
Details of the plan:	Keep Notes, Memos, Daily Info Log, Meeting Minutes, Training for Employees, Employee Manual.

Action Plan

Goals and Objectives: **Specific Dates:**

Action: **Specific Dates:**

Follow-up Plan: **Specific Dates:**

- What, how, when, who, why, what? Be specific!
- Client sets goals and objectives. Coach and client work on an action plan.
- The plan may have to be adjusted is something is not working, be flexible.

These are the original Twelve Steps as published by Alcoholics Anonymous

1. We admitted we were powerless over alcohol - that our lives had become unmanageable.
2. Came to believe that a Power greater than ourselves could restore us to sanity.
3. Made a decision to turn our will and our lives over to the care of God as we understood Him.
4. Made a searching and fearless moral inventory of ourselves.
5. Admitted to God, to ourselves, and to another human being the exact nature of our wrongs.
6. Were entirely ready to have God remove all these defects of character.
7. Humbly asked Him to remove our shortcomings.
8. Made a list of all persons we had harmed, and became willing to make amends to them all.
9. Made direct amends to such people wherever possible, except when to do so would injure them or others.
10. Continued to take personal inventory, and when we were wrong, promptly admitted it.
11. Sought through prayer and meditation to improve our conscious contact with God as we understood Him, praying only for knowledge of His will for us and the power to carry that out.
12. Having had a spiritual awakening as the result of these steps, we tried to carry this message to alcoholics, and to practice these principles in all our affairs.

The Twelve Steps in Their Simplest Form.

Step 1 Gives us the problem	Step 7 Action Step
Step 2 Gives us the solution	Step 8 action Step
Step 3 A decision to live in the solution	Step 9 Action Step
Step 4 Action Step	Step 10 Growth & Maintenance Step
Step 5 Action Step	Step 11 Growth & Maintenance step
Step 6 Action Step	Step 12 Growth & Maintenance step

The Disease of Addiction and Diagrams on Addiction and Recovery:

Below is an example of addiction. It starts with the big lie that allows addicts to use again despite all the negative consequences that have happened as a result of using, this is centered in the mind. Then the addict puts the chemicals into their body and they lose the power of choice. This then causes hopelessness. The ends to addiction are described in the bottom diagram.

_____

Assume that the family does not know what addiction is. Explain addiction in its simplest form.

This is a diagram of a normal person.

This is a diagram of an addict or alcoholic.
Because the spirit is blocked in the addicted person, the basic instincts become out of balance:

Because the basic instincts are out of balance the addict has fears, harms, and (resentments which are a form of anger.)

Circle of Influence

LAST 6 　　　　　MONTHS　　　CURRENT　　　TOXIC PEOPLE

　　　　　　　　_____　　_____　　_____
　　　　　　　　_____　　_____　　_____
　　　　　　　　_____　　_____　　_____
　　　　　　　　_____　　_____　　_____
　　　　　　　　_____　　_____　　_____

Positive and Negative Traits

+   **−**

_____   _____

_____   _____

_____   _____

_____   _____

_____   _____

_____   _____

_____   _____

_____   _____

Personal Timeline

Please write all positive life events above the line and negative events below the line.

Age 5_____NOW

Bucket List

Things I want to Accomplish During My Life

1._____

2._____

3._____

4._____

5._____

6._____

7._____

8._____

9._____

10._____

Ideas:
Skydive
Swim with Dolphins
Buy a House
Fall in Love
Be A Champion at Something
Save a Rescue Dog

Personal Stress Scale

We all have stress. Each individual demonstrates stress in different ways. The inability to cope is expressed in thinking, behaviors, and feelings. If you can rate and identify your stress, it can help you cope with stress in the future.

On a scale of 1-10 how often does your thinking get affected by Stress? _____
Behaviors? _____
Feelings? _____

Try to identify some of your stress signals:

Not Eating	Depressed	Crying	Nausea	Fatigue	High Blood Pressure
Tension	No Interest	Poor Concentration	Rigid	Bored	Memory Problems
Hopelessness	Apathy	Sadness	Helpless	Restless	Anxiety

How can you improve your stress coping skills?

GAF SCALE
---.
1   2   3   4   5   6   7   8   9   10

My Gratitude List

The people, places, and things that I am grateful for today are:

1. _____
2. _____
3. _____
4. _____
5. _____
6. _____
7. _____
8. _____
9. _____
10. _____
11. _____
12. _____
13. _____
14. _____
15. _____
16. _____

WHO AM I?

1. _____
2. _____
3. _____
4. _____
5. _____
6. _____
7. _____
8. _____
9. _____
10. _____
11. _____
12. _____

I AM _____.

I

Write a Good-bye Letter to Your Addiction

_____/_____/_____

Dear Addiction:

---.

Sincerely,

Goal Setting

The client always sets the goal!

Okay, so you're stuck and can't figure out what your goal should be.
Your coach can help you through powerful questioning and active listening.

1. Coach asks, "What is the most important problem for you to solve in your life today?"

2. Coach asks, "What will happen if you don't solve that problem today?"

3. Client should now answer both questions, while the coach listens to the client's answers.

4. The client should be able to figure out their goal based on these two great coaching questions.

   Remember coach, use open-ended, powerful questions here!

   This should help to remove the block that the client has in setting the goal that they need to reach a solution in their life.

Celebrate All the Victories!

It doesn't matter if the progress is big or small, celebrate the wins.

You don't have to throw a giant party, but acknowledge the progress in some positive way.

Think of ten ways the coach and client can celebrate progress together. Consider the first five as smaller wins and the next five as the "big wins!"

<u>Celebrating Victories</u>

1._____

2._____

3._____

4._____

5._____

<u>Bigger Wins!</u>

6._____

7._____

8._____

9._____

10._____

Random Acts of Kindness

Think of one act of kindness that you can do without anyone but you knowing each day for the next seven days. Write each act for each day down below and discuss with your coach at the end of the week.

Monday's Act was _____.

Tuesday's Act was _____.

Wednesday's Act was _____.

Thursday's Act was _____.

Friday's Act was _____.

Saturday's Act was _____.

Sunday's Act was _____.

At the end of the week discuss your random acts of kindness and how it made you feel with your coach.

Hero

My hero is _____.

The positive traits I like about my hero are:

1. _____
2. _____
3. _____
4. _____
5. _____

The positive traits I like about myself are:

1. _____
2. _____
3. _____
4. _____
5. _____

The things I need to improve on are:

1. _____
2. _____
3. _____
4. _____
5. _____

If I were?

> Think about what famous person, super Hero, or Cartoon Character you think you are most like and why?

Write down your answer: _____.

Why?
_____
_____
_____
_____
_____
_____
_____
_____
_____
_____
_____
_____.

NOTES:

Life Impact:

Who made the biggest impact in your life?

Family Members: _____
_____.

Friends: _____
_____.

Community: _____
_____.

Comments: _____
_____.

Treat Yourself Better Exercise

How well do you treat yourself?

Do you think that you deserve good things, fun times, are you nice to yourself?

A great way to improve self-esteem is to learn to love yourself, appreciate yourself, and do things that will make you happy!

You are going to plan a "you" day, where you will be very kind and nice to yourself! You get to do what you want to do, it's your day! Plan fun things that you love to do, cater to yourself, don't hold back, you're worth it!

Plan out your day.
Here is an example:

Breakfast at your favorite diner
A massage at the Spa
Shopping for a new outfit
Visiting an old friend
Lunch with your friend at a favorite restaurant
An afternoon movie
A bubble bath at home
Reading a favorite book by the fire

Be great to yourself, it's your day!

Insomnia Due to Anxiety Exercise

Take control of your anxiety!
You're awake anyway so get up for ten minutes.
Make a list of the top ten tasks that you need to accomplish.
Make sure that you didn't forget anything!

My Ten Minute Take Control List

1. _____
2. _____
3. _____
4. _____
5. _____
6. _____
7. _____
8. _____
9. _____
10. _____

Self-esteem Collage Board

Many people forget about their dreams, goals, hopes, abilities, and talents! Some people let other's block them with negative and hurtful comments.

This exercise is to remind you of who you really are and where you're really headed!

You will be making a value collage to hang on your wall.
Purchase a large poster board
Get together a bunch of magazines to go through
When you look through the magazines, search for pictures that represent your abilities, talents, goals, etc.

This will help you remember who you really are and where you really are headed.

My Self-esteem Calendar

In each block write down one thing that you like to do. Each block represents one day. Just one small thing that you would like to do for you each day. You can either draw a picture of the activity or write it down in the box that represents the day. For example, if you want to spend the day in the park with your dog, you can draw a picture of your dog in the block for the day that you would like to take your dog to the park or simply write it down in the block.

It's important that you make a commitment to yourself to check your self-esteem calendar every day to see what activity you have planned for yourself that day and follow through with it. You'll be glad that you did!

Sun	Mon	Tue	Wed	Thu	Fri	Sat

Confidence Building Exercise

1. _____
   Name

2. **<u>My Skills:</u>**

   _____
   _____
   _____
   _____
   _____
   _____
   _____
   _____
   _____

3. **<u>My Ambitions:</u>**

   _____
   _____
   _____
   _____
   _____
   _____
   _____
   _____
   _____

   ACTION BREEDS CONFIDENCE & COURAGE.

4. **<u>What am I or will I be Famous for?</u>**

   _____
   _____
   _____
   _____.

Resources

Dual Recovery Anonymous: http://draonline.org/
Heroin Anonymous: http://www.heroin-anonymous.org/haws/index.html.
Marijuana Anonymous: http://www.marijuana-anonymous.org/.
Methadone Anonymous Support: http://www.methadonesupport.org/.
Narcotics Anonymous: http://www.na.org/.
Naranon: http://www.nar-anon.org/Nar-Anon/Nar-Anon_Home.html
Nicotine Anonymous: http://www.nicotine-anonymous.org/.
Pills Anonymous: http://www.pillsanonymous.org/.
Sober 24: http://www.sober24.com/
Adult Children of Alcoholics (ACOA): http://www.adultchildren.org/
Alanon; Alateen: http://www.al-anon.alateen.org/
Alcoholics Anonymous: http://www.aa.org/.
Cocaine Anonymous: http://www.ca.org/.
Crystal Meth Anonymous: http://www.crystalmeth.org/.
Double Trouble in Recovery: http://www.doubletroubleinrecovery.org/
The National Council on Problem Gambling
730 11th St, NW, Ste 601
Washington, DC 20001
Phone 202.547.9204
Fax 202.547.9206
1-800-522-4700 Helpline
ncpg@ncpgambling.org
www.brunswickcompanies.com (Insurance for Coaching)

You should stay on top of current trends of legal and illicit drug use.
For Information on Chemicals, Drug history go to:
 www. Erowid.org
www.drugs.com (Pill Identifier)
www.streetdrugs.org
For Legal Forms and Contracts:
www.lawdepot.com
www.rocketlawyer.com
www.docracy.com
- ✓ Vistaprint worth visiting for business cards, and much, much more!
- ✓ www.vistaprint.com

Community Resources
*Build a network of local people in your area to network with and rely on to refer your clients.
Investigate your resources and learn which ones are the best in their field.
a. Medical professionals (MD, PHD)/ Clergy
b. Therapists/counselors/pastoral counselors
c. Interventionists / Anger Management Specialists
d. Psychologists vs. Psychiatrists
e. AA/NA community
f. Alternative medicine
g. Attorneys
h. Advocates

> *Over time you will build a list of contacts and resources such as detox centers, residential* facilities, outpatient facilities, sober houses, judicial, parole and probation, social services, etc.

Rev. Dr. Kevin T. Coughlin PhD Founder, CEO, President
Phase II Christian Coaching, LLC Email: ktc1961@ptd.net Recovery Coaching/ Family Recovery Coaching, Anger Management, Sober Living, Interventions, Speaking Engagements. www.theaddiction.expert 888-483-3017

Families Anonymous

For Relatives and Friends Concerned About the Use of Drugs
or Related Behavioral Problems
FAMILIES ANONYMOUS, INC. • 701 Lee Street, Suite 670, Des Plaines, IL 60016 www.FamiliesAnonymous.org

Dr. Cali Estes: M.S., ICADC, CAP, CPT, CYT
Founder, CEO, President
800-706-0318
CALI@THEADDICTIONSCOACH.COM
The Addictions Academy
www.theaddictionsacademy.com

Rev. Dr. Kevin T. Coughlin Ph.D. Publication Credits

KTC Publishing Phase IIC Coaching, LLC Amazon.com *Addictions: What All Parents Need to Know to Survive the Drug Epidemic.* 2016 Made the Amazon.com Top 100 Best Seller list.

KTC Publishing Phase IIC Coaching, LLC Amazon.com *If You Want What We Have; A Journey Through the Twelve Steps of Recovery Workbook and Manual* 2015 Made the Amazon.com Top 100 Best Seller list.

KTC Publishing Phase IIC Coaching, LLC Amazon.com *In The Sunlight of the Spirit* Workbook and Manual 2015

KTC Publishing Phase IIC Coaching, LLC Amazon.com *We Can; A Collection of Poetry, A Journey Through Addiction and Recovery 2016*

KTC Publishing Phase IIC Coaching, LLC Amazon.com *We Can 2; A Collection of Poetry, A Journey Through Addiction and Recovery 2016*

Tumbleweeds; Feather Books Poetry Series a Book of Poetry Written by Rev. Kevin T. Coughlin Feather Books England May 2002 (In Memory of DeWitt)

Wayne Independent Newspaper Honesdale, PA
News Eagle, Hawley, PA
Reading Eagle, Reading, PA Berks & Beyond
www.addictsrehab.com
BBS Radio Poetry reading
Blog Talk Radio - Interviews
The Serenity Show - Interview
Passion Diva Radio- Interview
www.sacredearthpartners.com - Interview
The Broken Brain (Blog Talk Radio) - Interview
www.eatingdisorderhope.com
Keys to Recovery Newspaper Beth Dewey CEO
www.keystorecovery.com
All 4 Ur Addiction Recovery Referral Resource Guide Jenny Clark Owner
Tripadvisor.com
MindBodyNetwork
Grieving Behind the Badge Peggy Sweeny Founder
www.theaddictsmom.com
In Recovery Magazine
The Sober World Magazine
The Soberworld.com
Shout My Book
Bookgoodies.com
Goodreads
Book Reader Magazine
Awesomegang.com
www.christiancoaches.com
NEWS CHANNEL 10 EYEWITNESS NEWS CHANNEL.COM
KHQQ6 ABC NEWS
ABC EYEWITNESS NEWS 8 KLKN-TV
FOX14 NEWS AT 9
Erie News Now
NTV Nebraska.TV ABC

Western Mass News Channels 3 ABC 40 Fox 6
ABC9 KTRE
7 KLTV ABC
Fox 19 Now
KXNEWC Eyewitness News
12 WSFA ABC
ABC 6 News WLNE TV
100.7 KFM BFM
Fox 5 KVVU-TV Local Los Vegas
13 WTHR COM Indians News ABC
Eyewitness News 3 WFSB.COM
Fox 12 Oregon
WDRB.COM
Fox29 WFFX.COM
WETV San Diego
HAWAII News Now
Marketers Media
WALB News 10 ABC
Tristate Update.com 13 News WOWK
AM760
WMBF ABC News
KCEN HD ABC KCENTV.COM
WECT6 ABC News
Eyewitness News3 WFSB.COM
WLOX ABC BOUNCE Eyewitness News
Eyewitness News 8
CBS8.COM
News channel 6 KAUZ
SPROUT News
12 Eyewitness News KFVS
KEYC MANKATO News 12 CBS & FOX LOCAL NEWS
3 WRCB TV ABC COM
KNDO 23 NBC
KNDU 25 NBC
The Aurorean, Encircle Publications 1998 Poetry and Essays
Joel's House Publications 1998-2005 Poetry and Essays
Our Journey 1998-2005 Poetry
The Poetry Explosion, The Pen 1999-2003 Poetry
Apostrophe 1998 Poetry
Nuthouse Twin Rivers Press 1998 Poetry
The National Library of Poetry 1998
Lines N' Rhymes 1998 Poetry
The Poetry Church Feather Books
England. Anthology John Hunt Publications 1999 Poetry
A Tapestry in Time. 1999 Poetry Book 18 Poems
Connecticut Department of Mental Health and Addiction Services
The Webster Times 1999 Poetry
The Angel News 1999 Poetry
The Skater won The Editor's Choice Award September 1999 (Our Journey)
The Blind Man's Rainbow 1999 Poetry

Arnazella 2001 Poetry
Feather Books, The Poetry Church 1998-2002
The American Dissident 2002 Poetry
The Good Shepherd Poetry 2002
Ya ' Sou Magazine Essays and Poetry
Colt. Winner Editor's Choice Award Contest Literally Horses 2002
Goodbye My Friend Read on the Radio Rhyme and Reason UBC Europe & the UK September 2001
Read on the Radio in Europe and the UK as a Tribute to those lost on September 11th bombings. My poem was read over the radio for many days.
Tumbleweed Read on BBC Radio in England 2001
Published by Feather Books
Notified by John Waddington Feather that Tumbleweed had been read on BBC Radio in England on Several Occasions.
Stanwich Congregational Flyer Poetry
University of Scranton Panuska College of Professionals Essay 2002
Scranton University 2002 Poetry
The River Reporter Newspaper 2002 Poetry
Unity Community News 2002 Poetry
The Poetry Corner Angelfire.com Poetry
The Poet's Market 2002 Poetry
The Poetry Church England 2003 Poetry
Cover of Wayne Independent News 2003 Poetry
Nomad's Choir 2003 Poetry
Written a series of 9 course manuals for a coaching recovery curriculum. 2014-2015
www.addictedminds.org 2015-2016 Articles Matthew Steiner
www.soberservices.com 2015 Articles
http://fromaddict2advocate.blogspot 2016 Articles Marilyn Davis
LinkedIn 2014-2016 Articles
Two Drops of Ink S.W. Biddulph 2015- 2016 Poetry/ Articles
The Addict's Mom 2016 Articles Blog
Ghostwriter Articles/ Content 2014-2016
KEITV12 : The Kingdom Hour- Interview

BlogTalkRadio The Kingdom Hour- Interview

About The Authors

Rev. Dr., Kevin T. Coughlin Ph.D., DCC, DDV, DD, IMAC, NCIP is an International Master Coach, trainer, best-selling author, writer, poet, speaker, a Diplomate Christian counselor, and therapist, he is Board Certified in Family, Developmental, Alcoholism, Substance Abuse, and Grief Counseling, the Reverend is a NCIP interventionist, a Domestic Violence Advocate, Associate Professor for DCU, a Provincial Superintendent (to be consecrated a Bishop in 2016) and so much more; he is an expert in the field of Addiction and Recovery. He was a Founder and Board Member of a Residential Recovery Facility New Beginning Ministry, Inc. and is President and CEO of Phase IIC Coaching, LLC., The Program Director for The Addictions Academy, and the Editor in Chief for Addicted Minds & Associates.

The Reverend has over forty-seven years of experience with the AA program. He has been working in the addiction recovery field for almost two decades, has helped thousands of individuals and their families overcome all types of addictions, substance abuse, alcoholism, process addiction, shame and guilt, relationship and communication problems, anger management, inner healing, self-image, interventions and much more. He is a published author and has published thousands of poems and articles published throughout the United States and other Nations, he has been interviewed on numerous radio talk shows, television, published in magazines, newspapers, books, and online publications; he has been featured on ABC, CBS, FOX, NBC, and the BBC in the UK. Rev. Kev is a former State, National & World-Champion Powerlifter, and still, holds several records. He loves to write, read, teach, listen to music, and spend time with people and dogs. His parents are his heroes.

Dr. Cali Estes, PhD, ICADC, MCAP, MAC, CYT.

With over twenty years' experience as an Addictions Counselor, Life Coach, and Wellness Coach, Cali Estes is currently serving as private practitioner working with a broad spectrum of clients. Cali has been featured on NBC Universal News, CBS Philadelphia, CNBC, CNN, Dr. Drew, HBO, CBS Chicago, Fox News, MSN Money, Yoga Digest, Entrepreneur, LA Times, The Fix, Max Sports and Fitness among many, for her work with Addictions and published in several journals and books with her work on ADD and Relationships and even food addiction. Cali has worked with the NBA, NFL, and MLB. Cali's multidimensional approach focuses on getting to the underlying cause of the problem and working in the present to combat her client's issues by creating a safe and secure environment for her clients to learn and grow and tackle life challenges. Her unique background blend of psychotherapy, life coaching, and wellness coaching allows the client to get to the underlying cause of their issues quicker, safer and produce results faster.

In addition to being a prominent therapist and coach, Cali Estes has presented at National conferences and is currently an International Education Provider. She founded The Addictions Academy and offers International Certifications and Courses in Recovery Coaching, Intervention, Anger Management, Food Addictions, Family Recovery Coaching and other Certifications to Professionals. She is a sought after Counselor, Addictions Coach, and Life Coach to Actors, Musicians, CEO's, Doctors, Sports Figures and Attorneys that need 100% Confidentiality.

Cali Estes is an interactive, solution-focused Master Addictions Counselor (MAC) and Master Certified Addiction Professional (MCAP), coach and mentor. Her therapeutic approach is to provide support and practical feedback to help clients effectively address personal life challenges. She integrates complementary methodologies and techniques to offer a highly personalized approach tailored to each client. With compassion and understanding, she works with each individual to help them build on their strengths and attain the personal growth they are committed to accomplishing. With 20 plus years in the addiction and personal development industry, Dr. Cali Estes is a trailblazer.

Education

PHD in Psychology and Life Coaching~ Master's Degree in CRJ ~ BA in Psychology ~ ICADC-Internationally Certified Alcohol and Drug Counselor LIC #709965CAP-Master Certified Addictions Professional LIC# 5349 ~Master Addictions Counselor (MAC) NCRC Nationally Certified Recovery Coach ~ CPT-Certified Personal Trainer ~CYT-Certified Yoga Teacher ~ Interventionist Practitioner ~ Life Coach ~Certified in Cognitive Behavioral Therapy~ Certified in Psychodrama ~ Public Speaker

See more info: www.theaddictionscoach.com and www.caliestes.com www.theaddictionsacademy.com 1.800.706.0318

Rev. Dr. Kev.'s Social Media Accounts

https://www.goodreads.com/author/show/14874631.Kevin_Coughlin
About.me Link: https://about.me/ktc1961/
http://ilikeebooks.com/if-you-want-what-we-have/
http://awesomegang.com
www.amazon.com/Rev.-Kevin-TCoughlin/e/B01AF6AAAI/ref=ntt_dp_epwbk_0
http://mybookplace.net/in-the-sunlight-of-the-spirit-a **Rev. Dr. Kev's Social Media Accounts**

Facebook
1. Kevin Coughlin: https://www.facebook.com/profile.php?id=100008449955607
2. My Group, Resources for those suffering from addiction and their families: https://www.facebook.com/groups/resourcesforthosesufferingfromaddiction/
3. RevKev The Addiction Expert: https://www.facebook.com/RevKev/?fref=ts

Linkedin
1. Rev. Dr. Kevin T. Coughlin PhD
   https://www.linkedin.com/in/revkevnetwork

Google+
1. Kevin Coughlin
   https://plus.google.com/112400908736308001821/posts
   My Group: The Recovery Community Family and Friends:
   https://plus.google.com/communities/113521225141112811207

Pinterest
1. Kevin Coughlin: https://www.pinterest.com/ktc1961/
2. My Group Board: Recovery We Can
   https://www.pinterest.com/ktc1961/recovery-we-can/

Tumblr
1. https://www.tumblr.com/blog/revkevsrecoveryworld

Instagram
theaddiction.expert

My Websites:
1. www.revkevsrecoveryworld.com
2. theaddiction.expert
3. theaddiction.guru
4. www.newbeginningmin.org

Rev. Kev's Goodreads Link:
-spirituality-training-manual-and-workbook-by-kevin-coughlin

Thank you for reading our work! If you enjoyed our workbook, would you consider reviewing it on Amazon.com? We would appreciate your help in getting the word out on how helpful this book is in both understanding coaching and activities for clients. Thank you so much!

Best of Life! Rev. Dr. Kev. & Dr. Cali